Releasing the Days

Releasing the Days

Stephen Meadows

Heyday, Berkeley, California

The publisher is grateful to contributors to Heyday's California Indian Publishing Program for the support that made this book possible.

Library of Congress Cataloging-in-Publication Data

Meadows, Stephen, 1949-
 Releasing the days / Stephen Meadows.
   p. cm.
 ISBN 978-1-59714-165-9 (pbk. : alk. paper)
 I. Title.
 PS3613.E153R45 2011
 811'.6—dc22

                              2011006651

Cover Design: Lorraine Rath
Interior Design/Typesetting: Rebecca LeGates
Printing and Binding: Thomson-Shore, Dexter, MI

Orders, inquiries, and correspondence should be addressed to:
            Heyday
            P.O. Box 9145, Berkeley, CA 94709
            (510) 549-3564, Fax (510) 549-1889
            www.heydaybooks.com

10 9 8 7 6 5 4 3 2 1

For my wife, Karly, and my son, Steve,
for their constant love and support of my work over the years

For Claude and Phyllis (Meadows) Smith, true lovers of Monterey
and of all things wild and beautiful

And for Linda Yamane and the Ohlone people,
past, present, and future

*I would like to thank Malcolm Margolin, Gayle Wattawa,
and Margaret Dubin, and everyone else at Heyday for making
this dream a reality. We are all into California.*

Contents

Releasing the Days

Peripheral Vision

The wind like this
the loose dunes
rolling
on below the cliff edge
the way the sea
taking over in its way
moves against the chrome sky

this wind returns the years to me
the friends to their places
on this stub of rock
passing a thin joint
while below in the sand hills
the tiniest plants cling
with the ocean and horizon
to an edge of this life

Waterhole

A reedy place
full of grasses
and tules
fronded
toad colored
by the bay's
curved edge
ancestors
accustomed to moist
pliant ground
came down
the long swale
for their water
a day at a time
stepping soft
in the wet mud
knowing
they would slip
just a little

Grass Valley

The dirt is red here
Stone speckles the ground
A light snow has fallen
in the night
The room smells of matches
Her husband is dying
She splits up the wood
in her bathrobe
morning by morning
releasing the days

Cosmology

Generations of spiders
weave their interminable worlds
among the rough cut boards
the hay colored chronicle
of bodies in the soft light
pendants of spirit
rivaling in abandon
the acrylics and oils on canvas
that speak to me of friends

In this room
with its colors spasmodic
over fifty some years
neither the sound of traffic
nor the rotting of the walls
nor the murmuring of poems
will halt this cosmology of gems
each delicate passed over body
a bright crypt in air

Norris Ranch

for Ken and Phyllis Norris

Red and yellow leaves
share afternoon light
each shadow on another
creating honey out of air
Flies are haphazard
their buzzing and the groan
of an icebox intermit
with calls from a small child
refusing to sleep
The sun in November just
an hour above the sea
watched over this ridge
through redwood and madrone
a ragged day passes
beyond the reach
of this poem
coming apart as the weblines
of a spider drift in
and out of view

In a Van Gogh December

The long broken limbs
of the greasewood
hang limp from the stove
My eyes burn and water
in the creosote smoke
that fills the small cabin
hot against winter chill

In the soil two years now
my father would have loved
today's cold clean blue
the wind howling wild
in the white writhe of poplar
the leaves letting go
into the wide wail of skyline
the yellow blood wheeling
out in great bursts
bereaving a worn wound

The Spirit of the Bayonet

You feel your feet
ride the dream
firm over the ground
You see only the tip of it
flash out in front of you
obscene and ancient
as the cruelty of war
The blue steel ahead
is an animal star
that glistens like death
over the hovel
of the world
The hands are precision
in this manner of worship
the aggravated ritual
of self abnegation
Eyes pouring hot
upon the cold point
impaling the red air

In the Final Hours
for Harold Meadows

You were killed
in the final hours
of the war
to end wars

As you bled
in the wire
you thought of your mother
your brother
you thought of the farm
the lush fields lovely
in the twilight
dew dampened
full of corn

There in the mud
you were so young
you left us no poems
you left us no remnant
no girl at home crying
not even the simple
sad eloquence of dawn
at your dying

In the Distance

Clouds swallow this image
of a half buried farm
In the foreground
a vacant eyed woman
grips the remnant
of a broom
Beside her a child
squats in tatters
unmindful of the storm
The curling steel pieces
of an old Ford
and entrails of box springs
commingle in the wind
In the distance a man
is knee deep in white dust
Holding tight to his coat
he is leaning
moving certainly away

Rena at 84
for Rena Meadows

Her pruned fingers turned
in the sun's soft blossom
eddying the way things will
that have lost the way to go
In this photo
she is in her rose dress
in her garden
by the hundred year house
where she gave birth to five
and has quietly forgotten
all the insults of a life
without losing the fine strand
of truth

Standing near a walnut
planted by her son
it is hard to believe that together
she and her husband
farmed fifty some years
while the buckboard gave way
to the auto
the auto to the moon

She stands here silent and smiling
in her favorite rose dress
the curves
in those bent hands
seeming to cradle the sun

The Burial

A scene one remembers
from a night full of dreams
The wet pit disguised
by a square of green cloth
Here and there small birds
forage in the grass
pecking to and fro
for each sad urgent seed
Beyond the white sand hills
comes the hard boom
of the rip surf
clubbing winter beach
Small fists of relatives
chat soft among the markers
relieved it is over
they are patterned like beads
about the nondescript stones
and the casket
incidental in the cold

At Noon with Han-shan

The pulverized dust
of the pasture
lies fallow at noon
Far outside the tree line
a train whistle gathers attention
in patient iron hands
Flies buzz and hover
in the cool silver shade
of these olive trees
caverned in the heat
The raw pungent odor
of horseshit and straw
wafts into this green cave
this place of concealment
where mad Chinese poets
chat lightly and laugh
about the rude broken boards
of my cabin
my agreeable song

Bare-Root

I planted the apricot
near an old peach
at the edge of this storm
that exhausts a worn month
placing the roots
into the earth just so
as if each had a predestined place
a warm sleeve in the soil

To allay these fears
that crowd close
in this dark
I revere now at all cost
the slow desperate days
toward the spring
that pull hope
out of the bark

Winter Work

Beneath a belly of cloud
cold ground
takes the clippings
The white breath of pruners
is smoke against the
stark apple branches
rooted dark into the air
A river dove calls
from a willow
Far out in the orchard
a ladder's faint rattle
the sharp purple clicks
of the shears like clocks
incrementally nipping
at the day

Nevada

Out here the bruised mountains
and a sun falling fast
just the sound
of those trucks
on the highway
these yellow leaves
sheltering
and the moon
a frail disc that is risen
half a purple world away

Snow Nearing Elko

The belly of the valley
into jubilant distance
cold crested ranges
becalmed by these flakes
up ahead the horizon
the stained Ruby Mountains
the sagebrush the gone trees
the stark flanks of foothills
the winded last light
and this pinwheeling whiteness
this freedom
overtaken by the dark

In the Bottoms

Down in the willows
the sound of a saxophone
meanders on a slight wind
up across the fields
the tentative sad notes blown
slowly over water
a blues that hits home
this night with you away
the country all around
bereft of reasons
and of thought
my own sense sifted
through that blue sax
under the black skies

Windows

In the room
rented out
to keep watch
over your days
windows on
the pines
fog moving in
over the hills
The nurses make
certain you can
unravel safely
dementia
after all
leaves us
nothing
the eyes
disconnected
from the soul
the breathing
green pines
outside
from their
dark
trunks rooted
now somewhere
in all of this mist

Abandon

for Eunice Meadows

Coming at you
like a threat
the long shadow
made by sunset
against the back fence
weeds and car parts
in the grainy
sad photo
your six year old
eyes looking out
of this cave
The Depression is here
your mom has run off
your father will die
of cancer
in ten short years
In your eyes
there is distance
you see past
the camera
as if a lone figure
stood calling
far away
down the road

Quietly out of the Way
for Richard Brautigan

At first light remorse
an ache in the room
the urge to weep
and with reason enough
and yet the knowledge
that by day's end
enough wine
all will be well again
Those ones on the corner
by the park
those ones in the weeds
as Brautigan said once
drinking quietly
out of the way
the world too much
too vacant
and nothing
for the pain

Blues for Juanito

for Juan Onésimo

No amenities but cheap wine
and those fits of weeping
the distempered wet look
of some dog and the black
cast stove picked up red hot
with a couple of burlap sacks
thrown smoking on the truck
when they moved you
to the corn crib shack

Son of old Manuel
far down on the ladder
of the children
it was always you and your brother
and the drunks from town
in beaten old cars that limped
through the summer dust
and shimmered in the heat
near the river

When you died on county sheets
of TB and too much wine
no more the soiled blanket
the broken cot crying
to yellow heaven in the heat

the few windows cracked
the lantern too
cracked
and remaining the tin shack
the bad sawhorse leaning
and the white alder
dead in the blackberry vines
like bone

Approaching Spring

Jays call
one another
through clean
winter light
cats roll
in wet leaves
amid piles
of horse dung
no work
and no poems
the sun
warm enough
to afford
even the failed
among us
pleasure

Outside
for Doug Bean

That last time
so frail
a rack of bones
hung
against the bed
the beard
since your illness
like weeds
filling spaces
where the cancer
had removed you
from within
Medicinal and quiet
I hear the clock
chime
I see the smoke climb
from the joint
as you doctored
your self
I can hear your words
thank me
can feel my soul
turn
the afternoon light

the sun
over the boats
in the harbor
the life
outside

Bert's Wake

for Bert Onésimo

I recall your face shining
You were fierce that day
behind the old John Deere
on the tongue
of that man killing scraper
Too young to help
I trailed you through the dust
Heard you grunt each time
you threw your body on the iron
Heard the cut sound
the earth made
the hard chuck of stones
and the wheeze of lung muscle
held against the live ground
Forty years of plowing
near that hog fence
laid a hill you moved
in a day
your work shirt stuck
to your black rubber neck
sweating wine

John's Song

At the end of the counter
the old man's falsetto quavers
brittle as his cup
some tune from the twenties
his voice a frayed reed
or the sound of bees
nesting in wood
It is his last October
Wrists about to let his hands
go the way of fruit
he does not lay them down
though they shake ever slightly
out of the sleeves
It is a song from the twenties
he moves as he sings
the way I've seen sick gulls
rocking in the wind
he does not care who watches
the white dusted fragment
of his body and the frail song mythic
and fragile as his sight

Faith in Words

Outside the crickets
beat on the still night air

close about the house
the not quite silence
the not yet redeemable promise
of life lived for words

the fog hangs low
in the alders cross river
obscuring the vision
the indistinct sound
of the water
the wetness of the sand

The Plow and the Stars

I work alone
in the greenish light
hand on the lever
that moves my blade
the quiet flakes
pour down through the beams
that probe a thin
column of this storm
In a darkened cab
only the eight hour night
spent shifting whiteness
into heaps here and there
From this mountain
the far city twinkles below
all thought here relinquished
given over to silence
and the snow

Bedtime Story

When I put you to bed
little boy
it is never without knowing
that you will not always be
a little boy
and when you're sleeping
and I kiss you
there in your dreams
a part of me
wants it all to stay
right here
your incremental breathing
and my wonder
and this bedroom
full of the moon

Fallen

Night dives
like an owl
the brown river
rises
he tends
the sad fire
a kind of
victory
in the rain
he mutters
placing
broken sticks
in homage
to this winter
where all
comes down
about him
dark
and storm

Faith

A cold hill
the leaves down
pine needles
drop
disconsolate
destitute
brown
in the news
all day world
economies fall
more talk
of another
depression
I sit here
quiet
in late
middle age
across the field
a woodpecker
raps
behind me
the moon
climbs out
of the pines
pulling in
the last
of the light

Manzanita

Smoke hugs the
hollows the
burn piles
these logged over
canyons
My boots crush
the silence
breaking up
crusted ice

I am hunting
manzanita

Lean bones of this
hard wood
make the hottest
of fires
At sundown
the memory not lost
picking up
scattered limbs
Like those ones
before me
I am living
fists tight
upon the song

Grandfather

for Roy Meadows

In hot dust
at field's edge
a rusted harrow
an old John Deere
buckets of oil
broken glass
at fence line
the dead grass
the thistles
of mid-July

Our heels up
on a porch rail
quiet roses
by the barn
cigar smoke
your hat back
you were telling
countless stories
about the old times
the river each spring

Alejandro

for Alejandro Onésimo

The close dark grain
of this antique chair
built about the time
you were born
holds for a moment
your face and its lines
entwining like the years
in my grandfather's field
a transient memory of you
your walk distinctive and measured
along the road
for wine and supper
looking as they all said
like a bear's in the shade
of live oak
you worked with the best of them
and had times been different
you might not have labored for wages
you might have had children
your signature practiced as a youth
more beautiful than my own
your untutored thoughts all those years
like the breathing of the oaks
the plummet and rustle
of an acorn
in a green quiet place

In the Water over Stones
for Isabel Meadows

Your voice Isabel
is a quail's voice
as the sun's song ticks
in the brush

It is the hawk's voice
and the heart's heat
of the rabbit
in the parched summer grass

Nearby in the river
in the water over stones
it is a willow voice
it is a crayfish voice
in the hollows
in the darkening places

At first light
it is the wind's voice
the mouth of the river
tule voice the voice
of a hundred breezes

The sun marks out
the red madrone

and in the canyons
it is a redwood voice
a sycamore voice
sweet scented

In the spring
it is the lupine voice
a blue white and purple
coverlet voice
all over the hills
and the meadows

On the river banks
as the set fires burn
and the steelhead run
it is the hunter's voice
flinging the gleamers
silver on the sand

Though the houses
of rich men now cover these hills
it is your spirit voice
your evening voice
your voice of the western waters

The stars hang out
over the point of wolves
on the edge of the world
the sea lions call

the otters break open
abalone

It is the voice of the land
It is the voice of bright shells
It is the voice of the valley
And the mountain Isabel

It is the voice of the people too

It is the weaver's voice
It is the young girl's voice
The gatherer's and the singer's
and the farmer's voice
the wives' and the children's
and the old woman's voice
It is the Indian voice
and the whalerman's voice
and the voice of the servant
escaping

It is the voice of your face
across the years Isabel
in my grandfather's face
in my father's face
and in my face as well

It is the voice
of the ones on the edges Isabel
It is the voice
of those ones with no voices

Hawk and rabbit
Quail and brush
Water and willow and crayfish and stone
Wind in the canyons
Daylight through limbs
The lupine the steelhead
The cookfire's call
Beans and tortillas
Your memories Isabel talking
Talking to us all

At the Grave of Richard Fariña

At the cemetery's edge
I came upon your grave
a simple peace sign
in the stone by your name
the gray wind moving
in the flowers nearby
the traffic imitating
the sound of waves

Startled by time
and what your prophecy
came to mean
I stand here to say
that your music is not lost
that your words rise up
against the obscenity of war
that your voice is not
locked in this hillside
unreckoned in the grass

Dawn

Lantern glow
on red wood
in the dark
outside
the slightest wind
in the leaves
the tiniest
change
in night
small birds
from hidden
places
hold
then let go
one by one
the language
of light

Eucalyptus

Torn orange bark
limbs littering
the road
we walk
the boy asking
about the trees
their medicinal
smell
I tell him
of past days
when I slept
in old trucks
and the groves
sent me down
enough branches
for a fire
every night

Looking Out

Time alone
makes for these poems
hours at my one small window
the charred color of rain cloud
rubbed into the notch
of the valley beyond
long days watching
as the storms move in
or listening at night
to the tune of the road
the distant taut hum
of heavy traffic on the bridge
the frigid stillness
of stars at five
before dawn

Sycamore

Outside the snow falls
around the sycamore trees
the street so quiet
the baby sings to himself
and sleeps in his warm bed
safe and unafraid
the yard growing white
under the gaunt wooden limbs
that are hands reaching up
out of the cold soil
imploring us to live

Faithful As a Body

The groceryman's light
in the dark like a bullet
against glass
low tide gumming
at the sand breaks
monotonous beyond
in the leaves along the street
the philosophy of flight
contentment unachieved
and aching in the ribs
the too much alcohol done
to the singsong of nerves
my coat of obscurity
faithful as a body
this night

Naturalist

My son
in the green
morning
light of the forest
prone amid needles
and bracken
his tiny hand
pointing
There in the cluster
of duff the small insect
moves with a purpose
through the chaos
of litter
I watch from above them
my young son
the insect
the rough track
through soil grains
and pollens
of springtime
the sound in the trees
of strong wind
above us
and above that
the startling blue

Blue Sundown   The Elephant Seals

for Breck Tyler
and Martha Brown

The last mating
battles now done
for this season
she burrows into sand
the carcass beside her
helps fend off
the cutting
spring wind

Losers here now
only eyeless pelts
these living ones wait
to reenter the swell
off Año Nuevo Island
In a few days
parting these waters again
she will feel
the bay's vastness
over the Monterey Trench
the green breathing breakers
that have long beaten
patience
into the rocks

November

One gull
spirals
above nude trees

the torn scape
of bottom land
ochre
in the wind

a lean river
rattles
over rock
into distance

worn water
winnowing
the sand

Above the American River

On a red dirt road
climbing the grade
into pines
Cloud on the ridges
in the higher Sierra
Below in black oak
a cold twist
of the river
Sun and slow shadow
snake and rock silence
the stark slanted peace
of the canyon

Still Life: The Plain at West Point

From dozens of buses
the not yet battalions
of chaste boys
approach the stone walls
youth in those voices
glib on the wet air
coats over the shoulders
careless as heroes
the hot July rain
from far down the Hudson
thunderheads blackening the distance

A still life that moves
that day's recollection
the green plain
the bleak river valley
the boys by the hundreds
enraptured
by the great stone gate
the first of them passing
out of sight into the dark
the rest of them following
following

Drought

Hot breath
on lupine
on sizzling
Sierra
parched grass
the seed pods
tick soft
in slow wind
on the skittle
this summer
madrones
are bright
yellow
ponderosa
brown needles
low water
sucks
the stone

The Clearing

Crickets once again
in the night outside
a sound like rushes
on the surface
of the air
a not quite monotonous
jazz
an incantatory
churning
On the edge
of this clearing
fog bending
over the house
the olive trees
silver
over the ground
wings among grasses
surrounding and conscious
in darkness
at the doorway
to dreams

For the Living

Standing high on this hillside
the wind off the Pacific
forming the language of grasses
and escarpment eternally speaking
the seabirds far out
on their planes of air
gather and squander
what the short days encompass
We make what we can
of what reason can give us
we take from these all too brief moments
some reckoning of meaning
hoping as we hurtle haphazard
through this storm of a cosmos
to make some small imprint
while the birds in their white realm
reeling over the tumbling green ocean
this plated earth gliding
beneath us like a wind
under shoulders
and the language we hear
in the grass on this hillside
is all of it mythic and wondrous
as the Goddesses dream

Reweaving the World Ohlone

for Linda Yamane

Enmeshing
with bone awl
with curved tooth
with dreaming
Again living patience
the slow walk
and choosing
The arms
and the fingers
of plants
the bent branches
the willow
the cattail
the root
the crisp grasses
The green limb
the gold stem
the soft flesh
the cleansing
the sheer thought
the taut hand
the earth's
whirling music
In your palm
in your lap

in your sphere
in your circle
This basket
this dance
upon the ground

Point Lobos

Our silence sings
we are the ones
born on this crescent
of rock and water
born of this light
friends of this sea
beneath these cool
constellations
The wind
in the pine boughs
sings our song
in stillness
we are listening
here beneath the trees
We are native
we were born
to rest among these stones
the roots and tongues
the quiet turned
among these bones

About the Author

Stephen Meadows is a Californian of pioneer and Ohlone descent. He has earned degrees from UC Santa Cruz, where he worked under National Book Award winner Lucille Clifton, and San Francisco State University, where poet Frances Mayes, the author of *Under the Tuscan Sun,* headed the Creative Writing Department. His poems have appeared in anthologies and journals nationwide, and one of them graces a bronze plaque in San Francisco. He has devoted much of his life to poetry, in an attempt to honor his ancestors and the beauty of the natural world. He is a twenty-year veteran of public radio, where he has interviewed scores of musicians and visionaries from the British Isles to North America. He has done all kinds of work to keep the poems coming and once, long ago, was even a West Point cadet. Stephen now resides with his family in the foothills of the Sierra Nevada.

HEYDAY
into California

About Heyday

Heyday is an independent, nonprofit publisher and unique cultural institution. We promote widespread awareness and celebration of California's many cultures, landscapes, and boundary-breaking ideas. Through our well-crafted books, public events, and innovative outreach programs we are building a vibrant community of readers, writers, and thinkers.

Thank You

It takes the collective effort of many to create a thriving literary culture. We are thankful to all the thoughtful people we have the privilege to engage with. Cheers to our writers, artists, editors, storytellers, designers, printers, bookstores, critics, cultural organizations, readers, and book lovers everywhere!

We are especially grateful for the generous funding we've received for our publications and programs during the past year from foundations and hundreds of individual donors. Major supporters include:

Anonymous; James Baechle; Bay Tree Fund; B.C.W. Trust III; S. D. Bechtel, Jr. Foundation; Barbara Jean and Fred Berensmeier; Berkeley Civic Arts Program and Civic Arts Commission; Joan Berman; Peter and Mimi Buckley; Lewis and Sheana Butler; California Council for the Humanities; California Indian Heritage Center Foundation; California State Library; California Wildlife Foundation/California Oak Foundation; Keith Campbell Foundation; Candelaria Foundation; John and Nancy Cassidy Family Foundation, through Silicon Valley Community Foundation; The Christensen Fund; Compton Foundation; Lawrence Crooks; Nik Dehejia; George and Kathleen Diskant; Donald and Janice Elliott, in honor of David Elliott, through

Getting Involved

To learn more about our publications, events, membership club, and other ways you can participate, please visit www.heydaybooks.com.